Drummane 2.0

DWIGHT DRUMMOND

Library of Congress Control Number: 2022901190

PAPERBACK: 978-1-957575-13-1
EBOOK: 978-1-957575-14-8

Ordering Information:

For orders and inquiries, please contact:
1-888-404-1388
www.goldtouchpress.com
book.orders@goldtouchpress.com

Printed in the United States of America

Contents

Drummane 2.0

Preface:
Drummane 2.0 is upgraded description of
success that's explain in Drummane.

Description:
Drummane 2.0 is a upgraded explanation of
success told in Drummane.

Technical Impartiality

Technology doesn't have any infrastructure of Black people;
who's ambition are impartial to the acts of injustice.

Rap Segregation

Every state should have their own Rap attraction;
which pushes the Music Industry to succeed beyond limited heights.

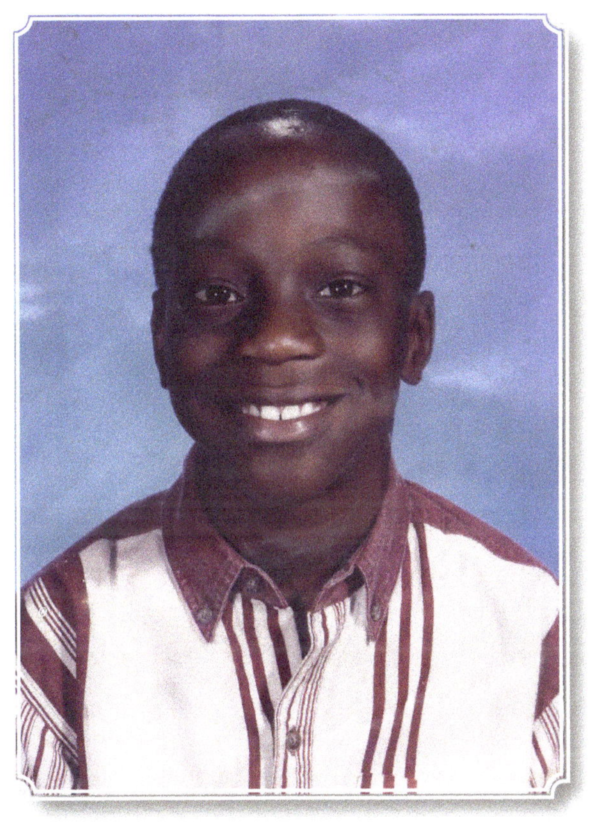

Drummane 2.0

Drummane is a laced faction tailored made success story
which pushes people to say "Drummane."

Black Dadeland. ll

In Dadeland where the inner city is unseen from sight;
though held in the light of upliftment. Which will soon be called
"Black Dadeland."

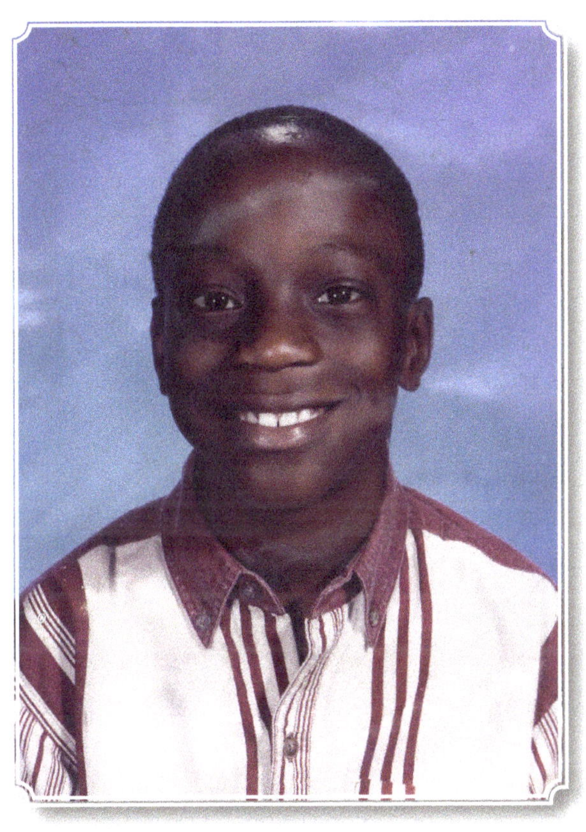

When a woman doesn't listen

When a woman doesn't listen it is seen
by reason that she is fed up with the man;
which control her daily choice of Love given by him.
Who realize that Love is eminent and needs to be
shared by a man and woman.

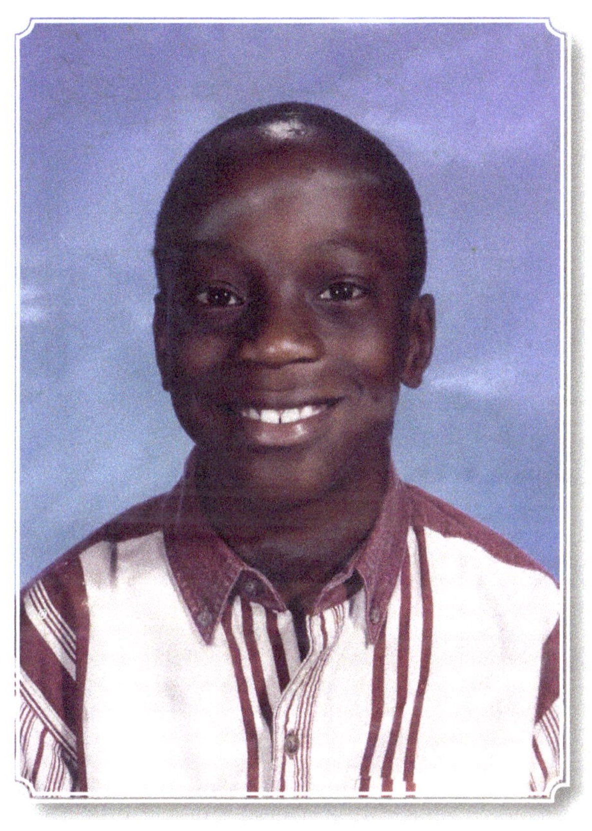

Widder 21.03. – 20.04.

Arie

A Aries born in the late 80's given a life of choice;
Blessed by God but given to the world as a man that will
slowly change into a success story.

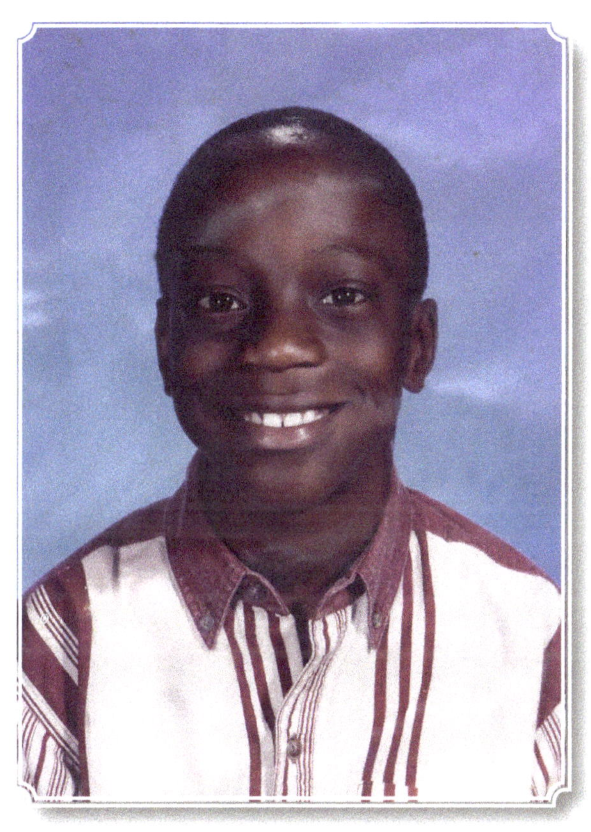

All women are the same

Some women may have wealth gilded by Life or a
man that can be passive to Life with issues; but who will
realize that a woman though different are all the same.

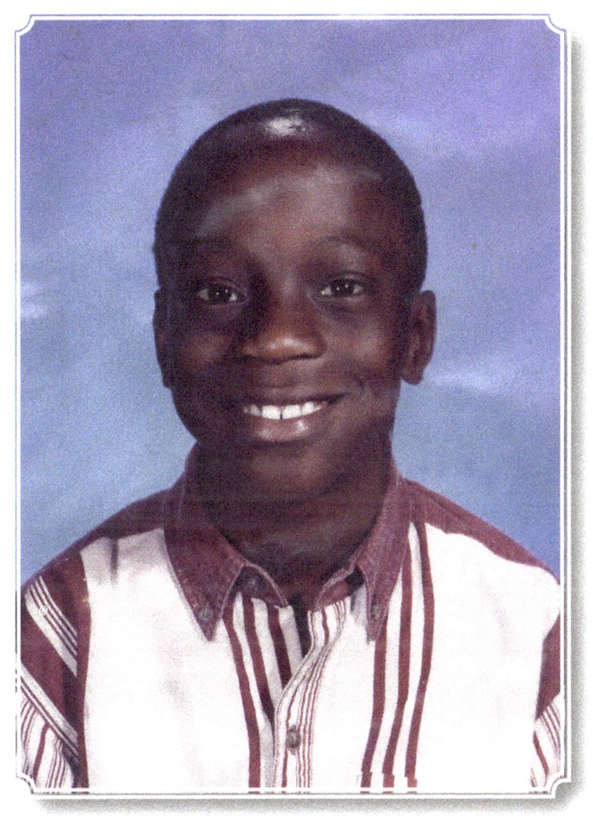

Black Cadillac

In a Black Cadillac truck Suv customize by the manufactured; success of any individual that is reliable enough to purchase it.

Reality Complex

Reality is a complex that isn't seen by man;
though blessed by choice no one will ever believe the realities that
Life bring except the individual man.

Black Lecture

Religion can confuse the reality that a person has of freedom; though Liberation excel all realities for Life which brings "Black Lecture."

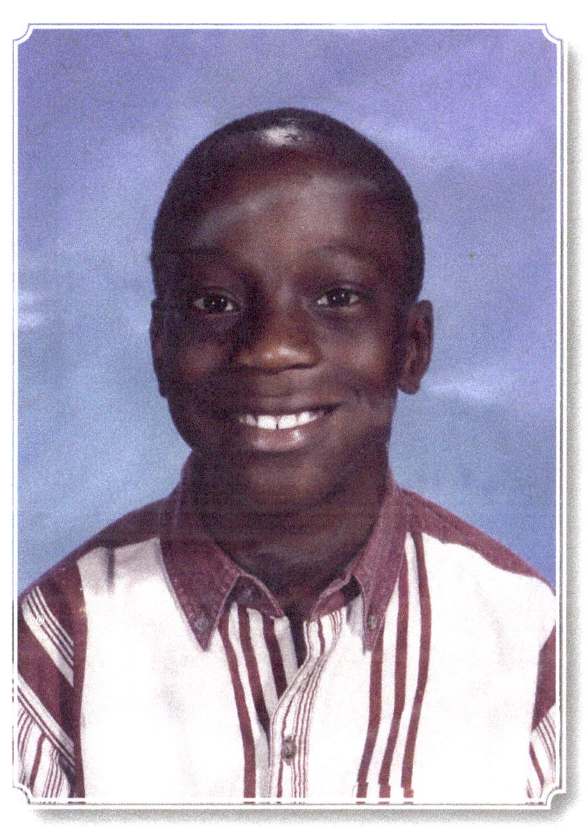

Love & Lucrative

Love can be Lucrative if a person realize success isn't successful without succession; who will realize that an individual can reason against anyone who doesn't understand. What a woman wants without the need of telling a man.

Black Trapeze

When a woman extends her body on a Trapeze from exercise;
will be the concept of Black woman.

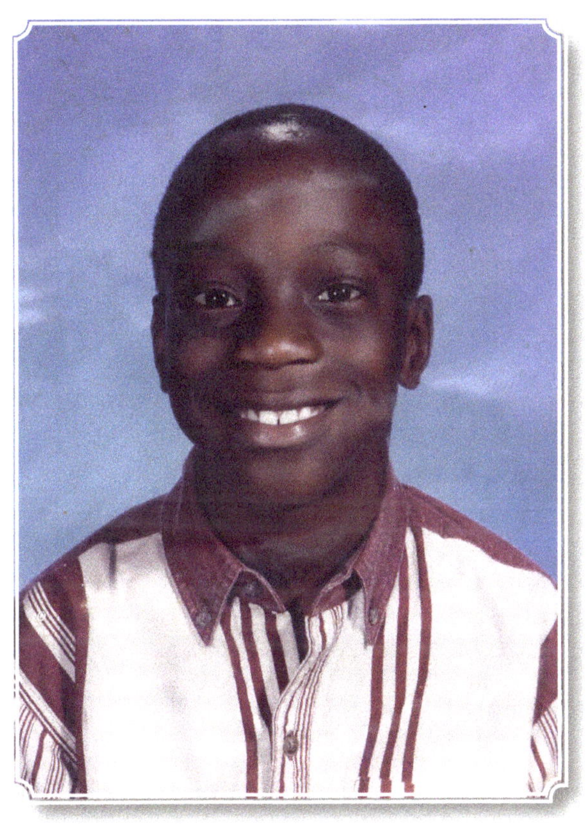

Jordan & James.

What is Jordan? Michael.
What is James? Lebron.

Basketball is a game that requires competition in the sport;
but when it comes to overall accomplishment it doesn't matter.
who is the best just the reality that they both played in the Game.

"Jordan & James."

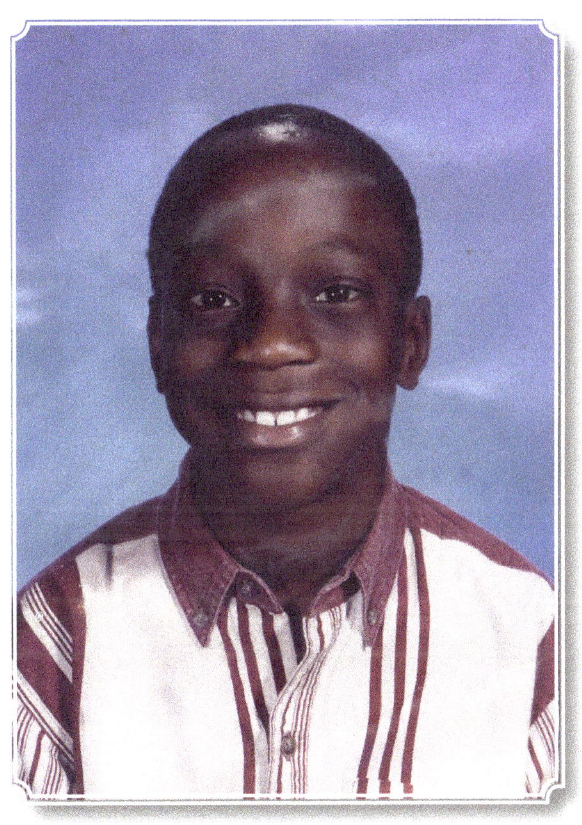

Black Clearwater. II

In Clearwater Florida where the privacy of any individual who loves to vacation on the beach; Enjoy the reality of Life but use all fun to be aware of the violence. Which plague the streets of night Life toward Black Americans near those areas.

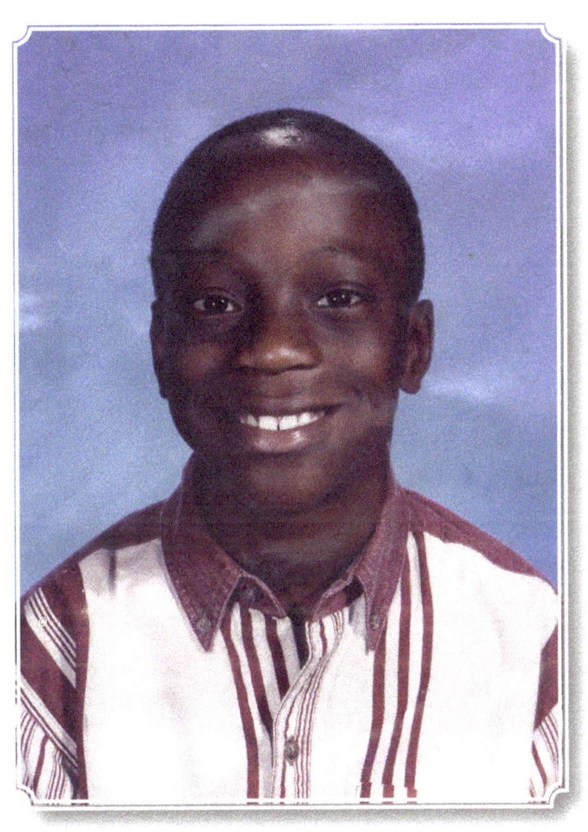

Domestic Liar

When a woman lies against a man unjustly saying
Domestic violence when everyone knows she is a liar.

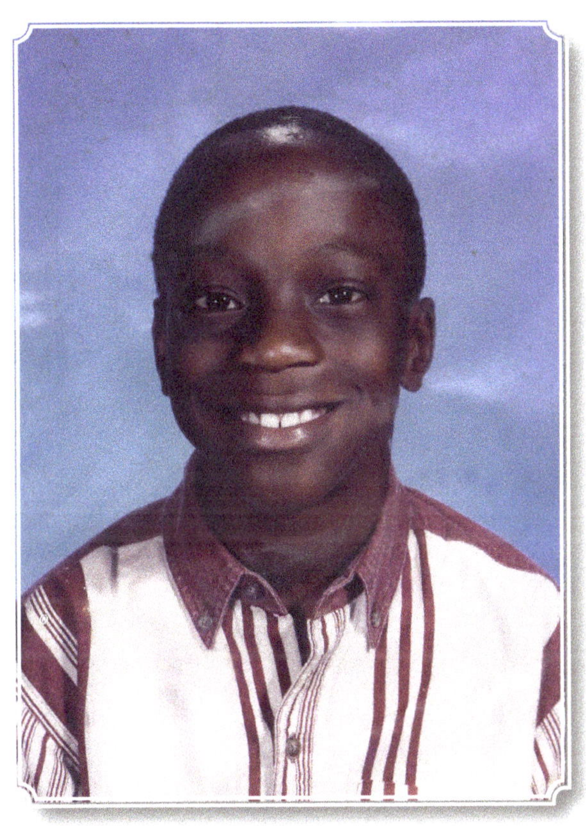

Black Versace

In Black and Versace unknowingly to all realities which pushes concepts to go unjust to acts of shame; When a person doesn't know how to treat a successful person who isn't seen in flashing lights of paparazzi cameras.

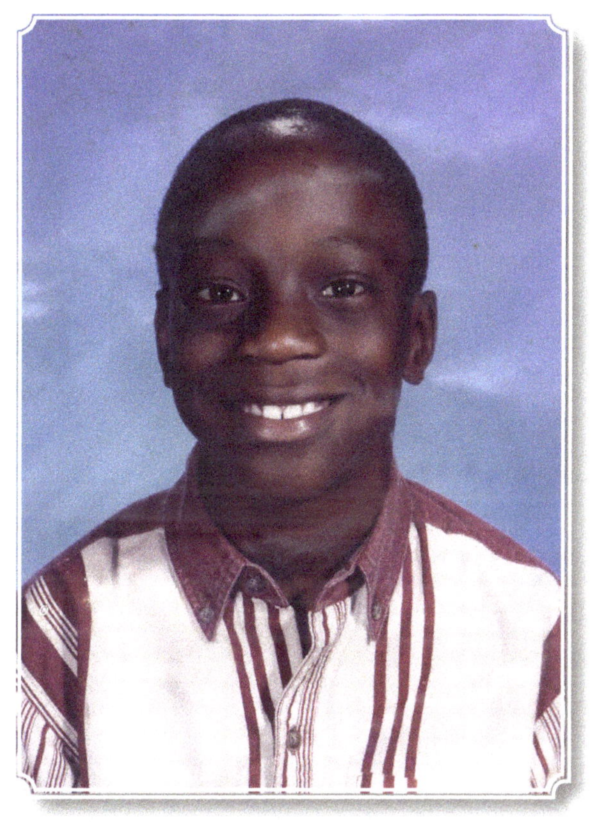

Violence against a Prostitute

Violence isn't necessary what a person
causes against a woman but it is written;
in the Bible that a woman shouldn't provoke a man to anger or provoke
the intention of kindness. Whenever a man is timid by life.

If I could turn back the hands of Rap

If I could turn back the hands of Rap selfishness wouldn't be glamorize by cause and justified by attacks from the media; who usually overlooks the importance of Black men that uses the importance of street poetry to dictate the issues of Life.

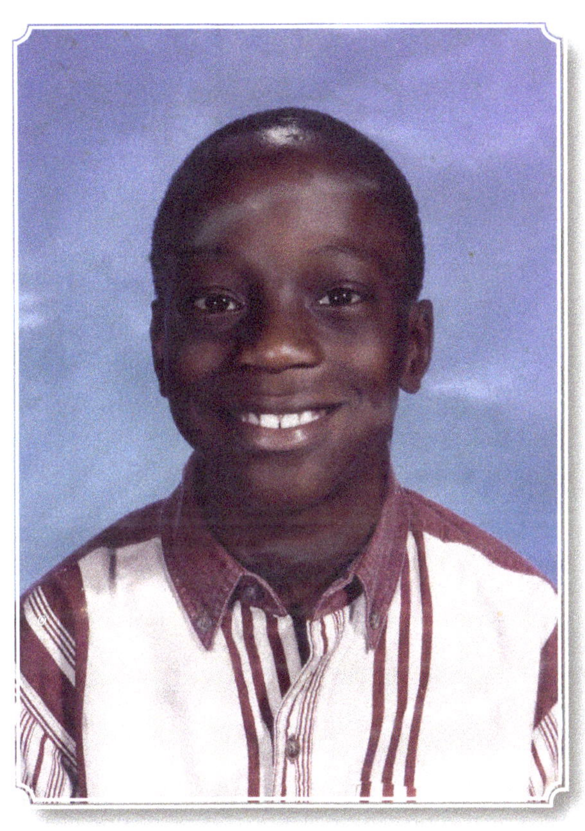

Black Indian

A black Indian woman; who causes a simple
Black man to fall for features
unjustly by reward of knowing she is Beautiful.

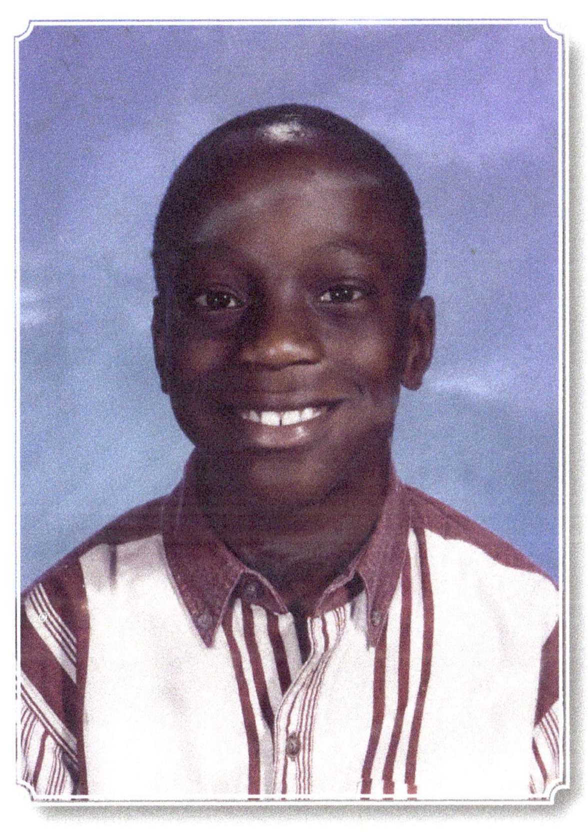

Some women are ungrateful

Some women are ungrateful but needed by men;
who love them but will never understand. What it is to be a man.

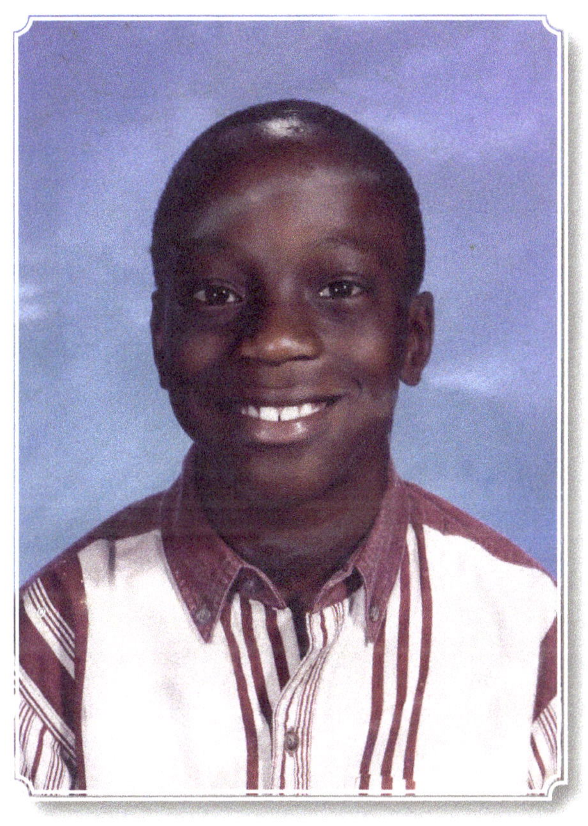

A Sisterly mistake

A Sisterly failure who by mistake use her mouth to unfortunately;
press charges against a man who is innocent.

"A Sisterly mistake."

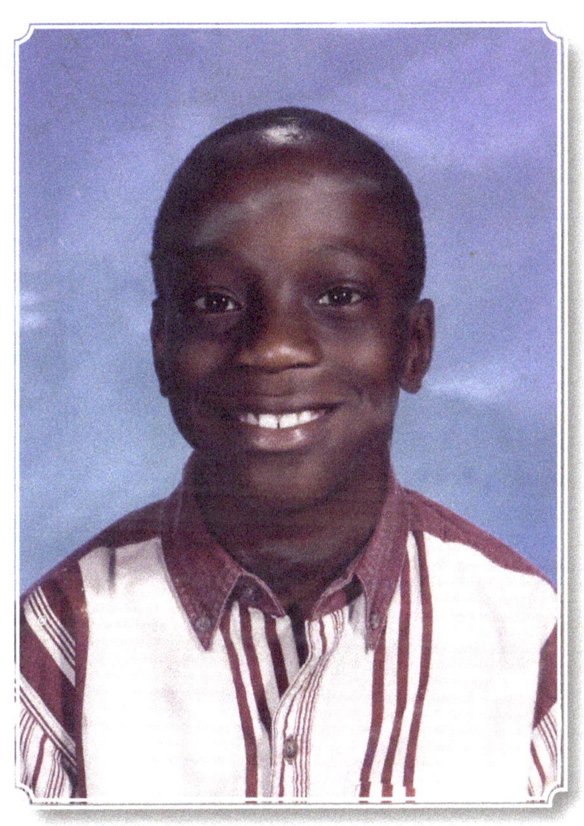

White satin

A White silk satin made garment customize for the cause of any man
who loves a woman.

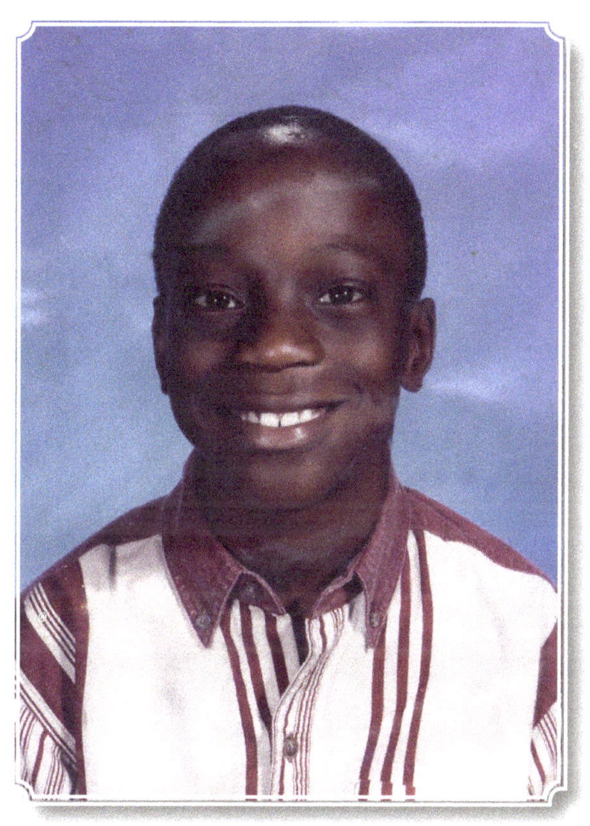

Rapfest

Rappers should have an event that broadcast them on a major scale a "Rapfest."

Herbs & Tofu

Herbs are manufactured and mixed into boiled Tofu;
which is made to taste so good as a Healthy man eats his daily meal.

Love is Essential

Love is Essential.
Love is Happy.
Love is mature.
Love is needed.
Love is Pure.
Love is Everything.

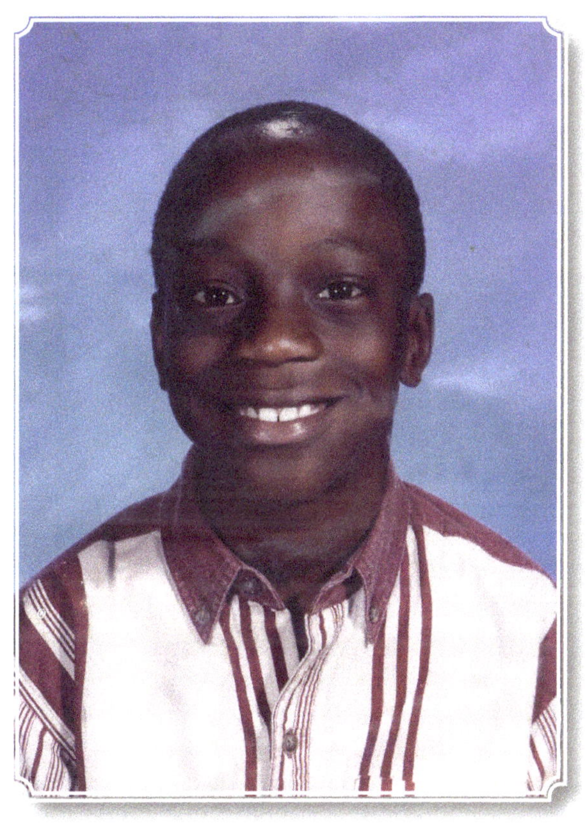

Library suite

In a Library books are written in typed manuscript of reason for
conclusion of fulfillment from Life issues.

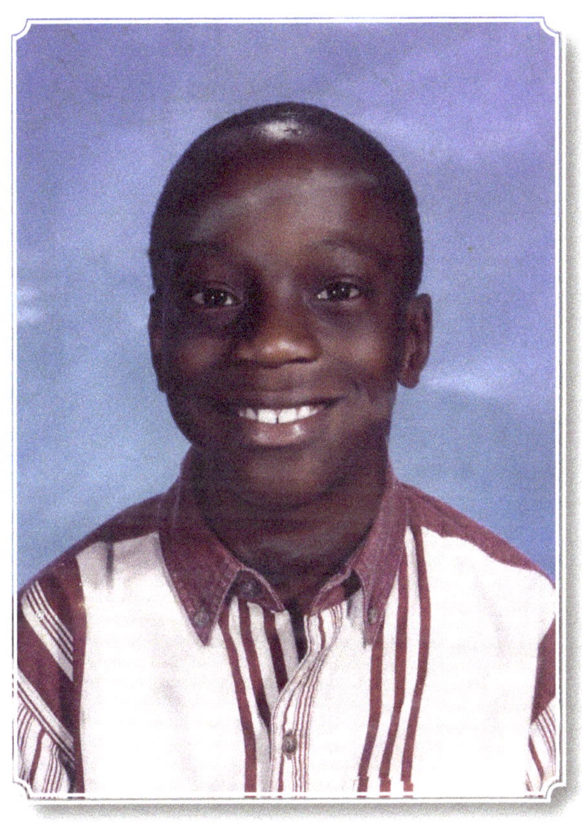

Literary Optimistic

Literary succession can be passed from generations of Authors;
which use their talents to be Optimistic to importers of Literature.

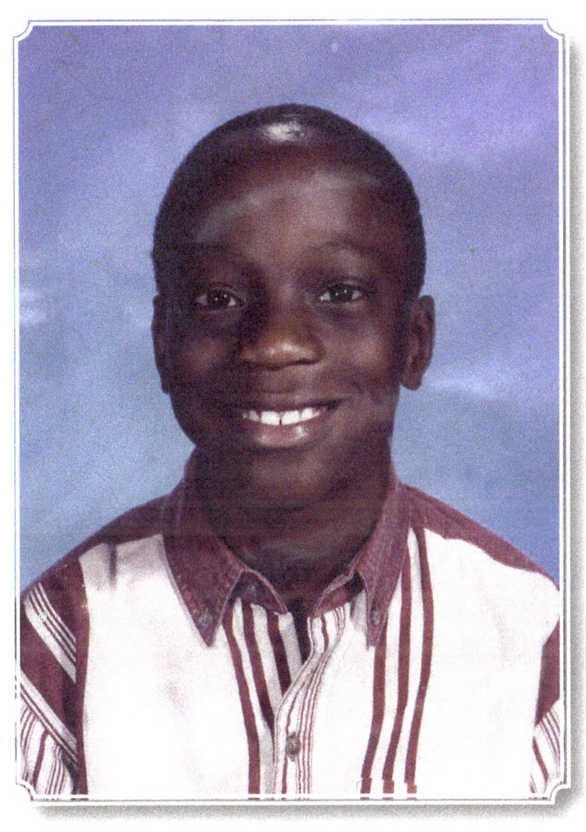

CHANGE

When things change

When things change the issues of Life;
will be overlooked and seen as lies which next existed.

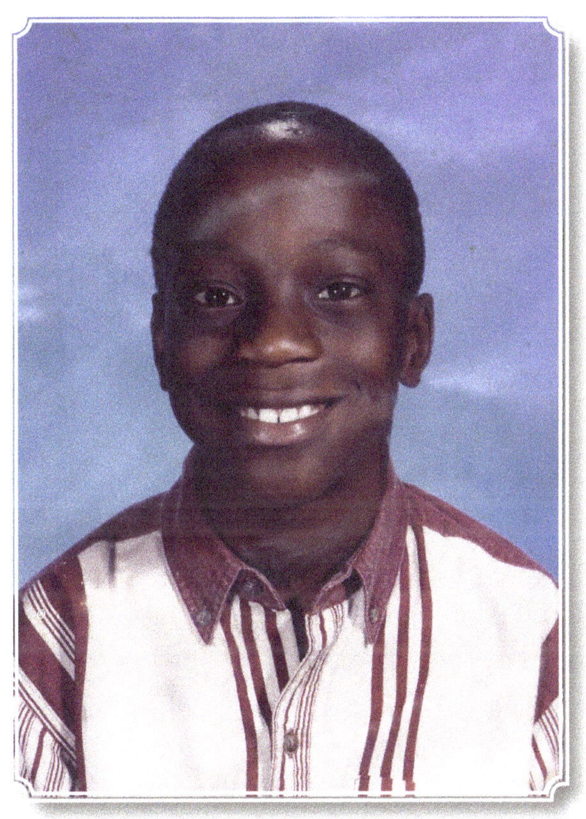

Religious & Musical

Religion pushes the need for any person;
who loves music to be unlike themselves but rewarded by success.

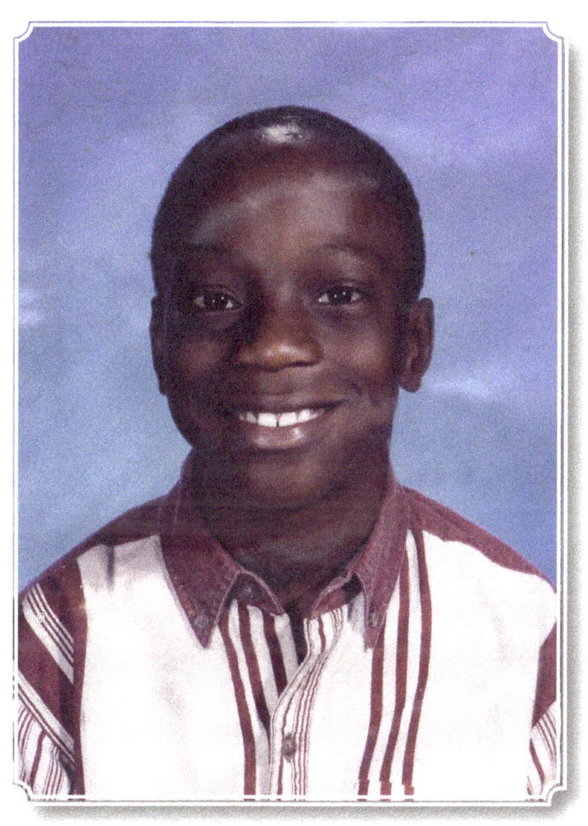

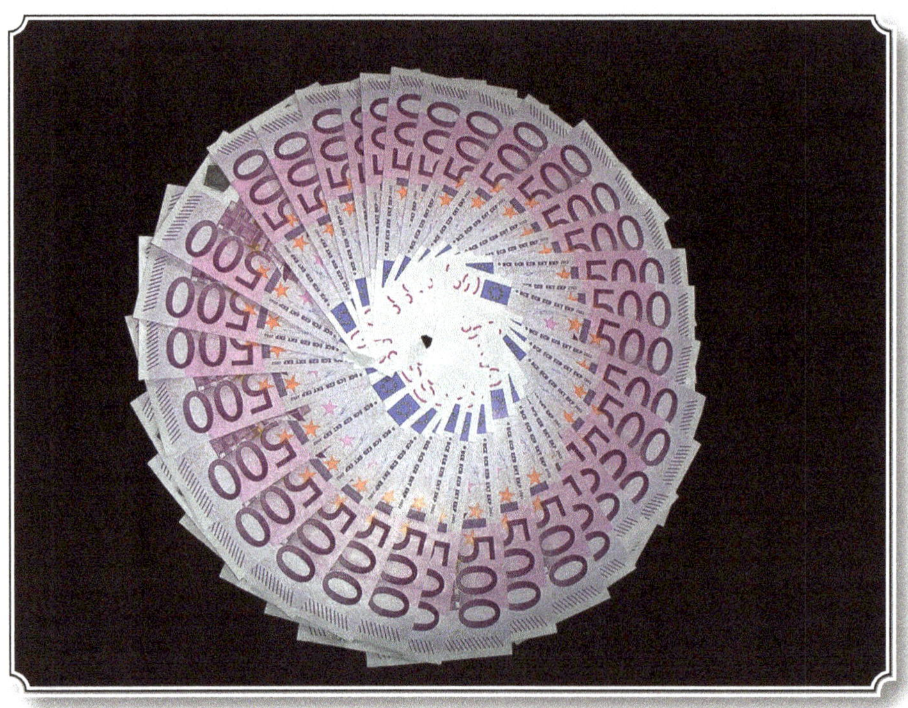

Grand Hundred

Gilded by ignorance the older generation doesn't know how to properly use those oppress by Life but Blessed in mere sight.

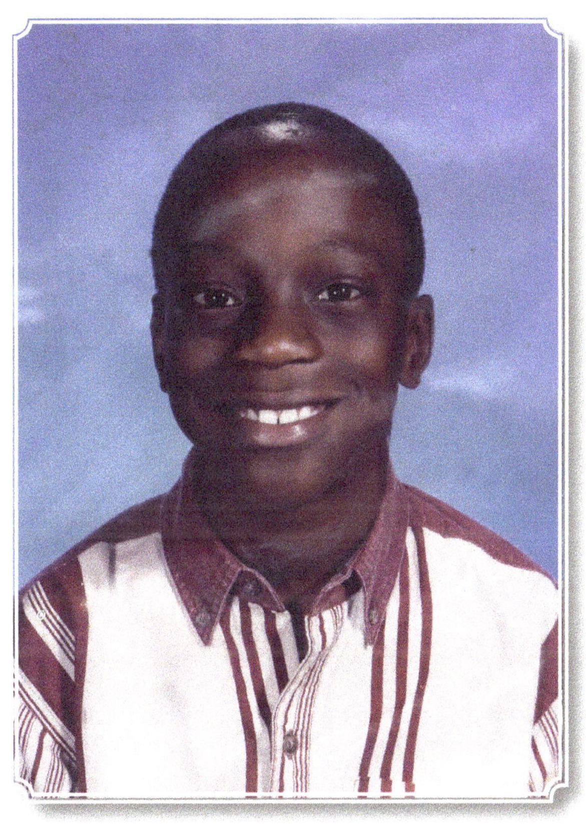

Acknowledgements.

I would like to first Thank God
for Blessing me with the Gift of Poetry.
Secondly I want to thank my Mother for being there.
Lastly I appreciate everyone that contributed to this Book.